CHADWICK BOSEMAN

Forever Our King | 1976-2020

MIA JOHNSON

TRIUMPH
B O O K S

No part of this publication may be reproduced, stored in a retrieval system, or transmitted in any form by any means, electronic, mechanical, photocopying, or otherwise, without the prior written permission of the publisher, Triumph Books LLC, 814 North Franklin Street, Chicago, Illinois 60610.

Library of Congress Cataloguing-in-Publication Data available upon request.

This book is available in quantity at special discounts for your group or organization. For further information, contact:

Triumph Books LLC
814 North Franklin Street
Chicago, Illinois 60610
(312) 337-0747
www.triumphbooks.com

Printed in U.S.A.

ISBN: 978-1-62937-830-5

Design and page production by Patricia Frey
Cover design by Jonathan Hahn

Cover photos courtesy of Getty Images

CONTENTS

1

To Be Young, Gifted, and Black

In the record-breaking 2018 movie *Black Panther*, Chadwick Boseman's character T'Challa (the Black Panther) meets his father on the ancestral plane. It's a realm where the spirits of those lost have their final resting place on the other side. Upon visiting the mysterious world for the first time, T'Challa is greeted by his father—who he's now in line to succeed on the throne. He tells his father, "I am not ready to be without you." It's a powerful line in the film, but one that few could have guessed would be so relevant in just a few years' time.

On August 28, 2020, the world learned that Chadwick Boseman had passed away at the age of 43. A man who had lived his life in the public eye kept a quiet battle against colon cancer private, and it left the world feeling like T'Challa: not ready to be without him.

Boseman's death had been announced on his social media platforms telling the story that very few people got to hear. His fight with cancer had stemmed back to 2016, where he received a stage III diagnosis. Nonetheless, the actor didn't let the news stop him from advancing in his career. He continued to act and make public appearances for the films he starred in—leaving his diagnosis unknown to everyone but his family. Even close colleagues had no idea of his condition, most learning about his struggle and his passing at the same time the social media post was shared.

The post also confirmed that Boseman had married his long-time partner, singer Taylor Simone Ledward. The two were first seen dating in 2015, but much of their relationship was kept private until the statement make their marriage public.

Chadwick Boseman attends the 2018 MTV Movie & TV Awards at Barker Hangar on June 16, 2018, in Santa Monica, California. (Emma McIntyre/Getty Images for MTV)

Chadwick Boseman ✔
@chadwickboseman

It is with immeasurable grief that we confirm the passing of Chadwick Boseman.

Chadwick was diagnosed with stage III colon cancer in 2016, and battled with it these last 4 years as it progressed to stage IV.

A true fighter, Chadwick persevered through it all, and brought you many of the films you have come to love so much. From *Marshall* to *Da 5 Bloods*, August Wilson's *Ma Rainey's Black Bottom* and several more, all were filmed during and between countless surgeries and chemotherapy.

It was the honor of his career to bring King T'Challa to life in *Black Panther*.

He died in his home, with his wife and family by his side.

The family thanks you for your love and prayers, and asks that you continue to respect their privacy during this difficult time.

9:11 PM • Aug. 28, 2020

The post was shared on both Instagram and Twitter and quickly received a lot of attention. The Instagram post as of this publishing has well over 18 million likes, making it one of the most-liked pictures on Instagram. And on Twitter, the announcement broke records as well. Collecting over 3 million retweets and 7.7 million likes, Twitter announced a day later that it had become the platform's most-liked tweet to date. Boseman's name began trending all over social media as fans, celebrities, and notable figures from all over paid their respects to Boseman online. And it's no wonder that the news of his passing received so much attention.

Boseman was not only a star with a brilliant résumé of films behind him, but he was so in demand that even after starring in *Black Panther*, he had many more projects to come.

Chadwick Boseman attends the *Get on Up* premiere at the Apollo Theater on July 21, 2014, in New York City. (Jemal Countess/Getty Images)

He had biopics such as *42*, *Get on Up*, and *Marshall* under his belt. He played Black Panther not just once in his solo movie, but also appearing in the megahits *Captain America: Civil War*, *Avengers: Infinity War*, and the No. 1 movie of all time, *Avengers: Endgame*.

Following those movies, Boseman starred in *21 Bridges* and Spike Lee's *Da 5 Bloods*. And he's even appeared in a wealth of television shows ranging from having parts in *Law & Order* and *CSI: NY* to hosting *Saturday Night Live*. Those few roles, of course, only scratch the surface of his life as an actor, but it shows just how much of an effect he's had on pop culture in recent years. Boseman even has a few projects that will now be released posthumously, including a film adaptation of the August Wilson play *Ma Rainey's Black Bottom* and a voice role in the animated Marvel series *What If…?*.

Needless to say, Boseman has solidified himself as a legend. And it all started with his dream of studying film as a young college student. Prior to beginning his studies, Boseman grew up in Anderson, South Carolina, born on November 29, 1976. It was when he attended high school that he made his first breakthrough in the world of entertainment. Back then, Boseman was on the school's basketball team. He was notably a great player, but his world as a young high school student was rocked when a friend and fellow teammate was shot and killed. As a way to process his feelings, Boseman wrote the play *Crossroads* and had it produced at his school in his friend's honor. After that, a spark was lit in Boseman that led him to a world of arts and entertainment.

For college, Boseman enrolled at Howard University, the Historically Black College in Washington, D.C. And

A Résumé Fit for a King

Movies

Ma Rainey's Black Bottom (2020)
Levee

Da 5 Bloods (2020)
Stormin' Norman

21 Bridges (2019)
Andre Davis

Avengers: Endgame (2019)
T'Challa / Black Panther

Avengers: Infinity War (2018)
T'Challa / Black Panther

Black Panther (2018)
T'Challa / Black Panther

Marshall (2017)
Thurgood Marshall

Message from the King (2016)
Jacob King

Captain America: Civil War (2016)
T'Challa / Black Panther

Gods of Egypt (2016)
Thoth

Get on Up (2014)
James Brown

Draft Day (2014)
Vontae Mack

42 (2013)
Jackie Robinson

The Kill Hole (2012)
Lt. Samuel Drake

The Express (2008)
Floyd Little

TV

Fringe (2011)
Cameron James

Justified (2011)
Ralph "Flex" Beeman

Detroit 1-8-7 (2011)
Tommy Westin

Castle (2011)
Chuck Russell

The Glades (2010)
Michael Richmond

Persons Unknown (2010)
Graham McNair

Lie to Me (2009)
Cabe McNeil

Lincoln Heights (2008)
Nathaniel Ray

Cold Case (2008)
Dexter "Dex" Collins '05

ER (2008)
Derek Taylor

CSI: NY (2006)
Rondo

Law & Order (2004)
Foster Keyes

Third Watch (2003)
David Wafer

All My Children (2003)
Reggie Porter Montgomery #1

though he's known for being an actor now, that wasn't exactly what Boseman had in mind when he was studying. In fact, the star received a Bachelor of Fine Arts in directing, but his education still allowed him to explore all facets of acting and storytelling—and he did so with some excellent help along the way.

One of his mentors at the time was *The Cosby Show* actress Phylicia Rashad. The Tony-winning actress was the instructor for one of his acting classes at Howard, and she very much enjoyed having Boseman as a student.

"What I saw in him was the sky was the limit," she told *Rolling Stone* in 2018. "He never asked me to introduce him to anyone—that's not his way. He was going to make it on his own merits."

Rashad even helped Boseman and a few of his classmates study abroad at Oxford University in England. There, he studied under a prestigious summer theater program that other actors such as Paul Rudd, Orlando Bloom, and David Schwimmer studied under. Though the program was a little pricey, Rashad was able to gather some assistance from a "celebrity friend" to help fund the trip. As Boseman later found out, that funding came from none other than Denzel Washington.

In a speech honoring Washington for the American Film Institute's Lifetime Achievement Award, Boseman said in 2019: "Imagine receiving the letter that your tuition for that summer was paid for and that your benefactor was none other than the dopest actor on the planet… There is no Black Panther without Denzel Washington."

Chadwick Boseman and Phylicia Rashad attend the 2015 Alvin Ailey Opening Night Benefit Gala at New York City Center on December 2, 2015, in New York City. (Johnny Nunez/WireImage)

But Denzel Washington and Phylicia Rashad weren't the only stars to have a positive effect on Boseman's life during college. The young student would come in contact with a future castmate who's another powerful name in acting: Angela Bassett. In the Marvel universe, Bassett plays Queen Ramonda, the mother of T'Challa who encourages him to be a strong king. Offscreen, their chemistry was just as strong, almost as if Boseman had received an additional maternal figure in his life with Bassett. After his passing, the actress shared a statement on social media revealing just how the two crossed paths years before working together on *Black Panther*. During his time in college, Bassett received an honorary degree from his university, Howard. And it just so happened that Boseman himself was selected to

Chadwick Boseman and Angela Bassett attend the Marvel Studios' *Black Panther* Global Junket Press Conference on January 30, 2018, in Beverly Hills, California. (Alberto E. Rodriguez/Getty Images for Disney)

escort the actress on that day. It was quite the charming story that she recalls him telling her at the premiere of *Black Panther*.

By the time Boseman was out of college, he moved to Brooklyn in New York and immersed himself in the theater world. As a new performer on the scene, he wasn't so much ready to hit Broadway, but he was something of a secret founding father when it came to one of Broadway's biggest hits: *Hamilton*. No, he's not tied to the musical himself. But Boseman teased that in his style of theater, he was doing what *Hamilton* did, only 15 years earlier. His goal at the time was to write and direct plays, some of which (like *Hamilton*) included using rap as a way to tell the story.

From there, Boseman took roles in plays, continued writing and directing

in his twenties, and eventually found his way to television. These days, it's not uncommon to see big-name stars who had parts on *Law & Order, CSI: NY,* and even *ER* before they made it big, and Boseman was lucky enough to add his name to that list.

After those roles, Boseman finally decided to make the move out to Los Angeles, when he landed a role in ABC's *Lincoln Heights* in 2008. It was a move that pushed him out of his comfort zone, as he was content to live in New York and continue under that scene. But as the saying goes, if you can make it in New York, you can make it anywhere. And so, Chadwick Boseman was on his way to making a name for himself in Hollywood.

Chadwick Boseman attends the 2012 Santa Barbara International Film Festival on January 28, 2012, in Santa Barbara, California. (Ray Mickshaw/WireImage)

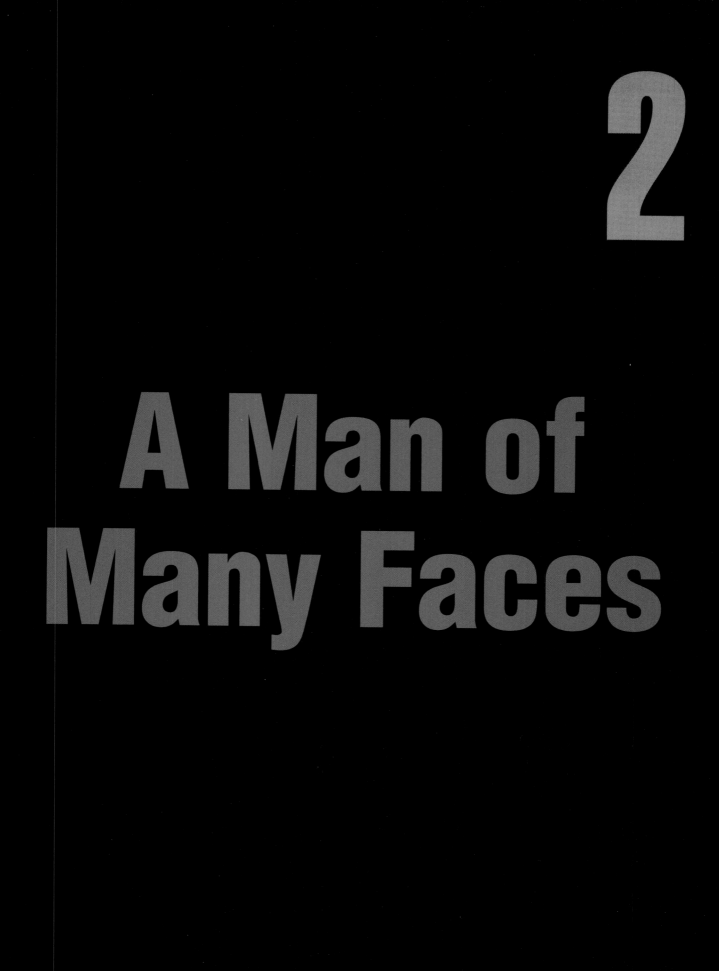

2

A Man of Many Faces

After heading to Hollywood, Chadwick Boseman's career took a tremendous upturn that began to thrust him into the spotlight. Before portraying three of America's biggest icons on film, Boseman was featured in two films, but nothing would compare to his first major lead role and the subsequent films that followed.

During his career, he knocked it out of the park playing the baseball legend Jackie Robinson in 2013's *42*, brought funk to the role of James Brown in 2014's *Get on Up*, and did justice to Thurgood Marshall while playing him in 2017's *Marshall*—three films that showed Boseman can be a man of many faces.

In fact, between playing these three legendary figures on top of playing the iconic Black Panther, many began to joke, who *couldn't* Chadwick Boseman play? Certainly, it felt like if there was any powerful Black role that could be played, Boseman was the man to do it. But of course, it all started with the movie *42*—a life-changing movie at that.

Knocking It Out of the Park

Although basketball was Boseman's sport of choice growing up, in his first major role he portrayed a legend on the field instead of a legend on the court. But Boseman, after all, was an actor, which meant he absolutely knew how to get in tune

Chadwick Boseman as Jackie Robinson in *42*. (Warner Bros./Photofest)

with the person he's playing to bring them to life on screen.

Now, we know that Boseman absolutely had what it took to bring someone like Jackie Robinson to life in a movie like *42*. And he can certainly hold his own in scenes with co-stars like Harrison Ford and Alan Tudyk. But back in 2014, he was still relatively new to the scene, and the world had a lot to learn about this soon-to-be king.

The writer and director of *42*, Brian Helgeland, told *The New York Times* in 2018 that he chose Boseman as the lead after seeing only two other auditions. Just from the auditions, he could feel that a star was being born. "It's the way he carries himself, his stillness—you just have that feeling that you're around a strong person," Helgeland said of Boseman in the interview.

If things had worked out differently (at a much different time) Boseman may have never gotten the role to begin with. Around 1995, Spike Lee was planning on directing and writing a movie based on Jackie Robinson. The film was eyeing Denzel Washington to take the lead role, and the release of the movie in 1997 would have celebrated the 50-year anniversary of Robinson breaking baseball's color barrier. The project

What Is the Color Barrier?

In baseball, the color barrier (also known as the color line) was a form of segregation that excluded Black players from playing in Major League Baseball. Jackie Robinson was the first Black player to break the color barrier in 1947 when he joined the Brooklyn Dodgers.

Chadwick Boseman shares a laugh with fellow cast member Harrison Ford at the Los Angeles premiere of *42* at the TCL Chinese Theater on April 9, 2013, in Los Angeles. (Chris Pizzello/Invision/AP)

was later abandoned due to creative differences, and it took quite a long time for a Jackie Robinson movie to be put into development again. By 2011, the Robinson biopic was revived, with Warner Bros. ultimately picking up the project.

When it came preparing for the role of Jackie Robinson, Boseman put all his effort into becoming a believable baseball star. All aspects of playing the sport were foreign to him, so it took a team to make sure that the actor could portray a professional baseball player and do it right.

"[It's] almost like learning a musical instrument at 30," said Nick Dingman, one of Boseman's trainers, to The Athletic. "It didn't discourage him."

That'll be a theme that will constantly show up in Boseman's story: the ability to keep going no matter what. For 42, Boseman even had the help of Jackie Robinson's wife, Rachel Robinson, to act as a fact-checker to make sure the movie was as accurate as possible.

With all the support behind him, Boseman focused on delivering both the dramatic scenes and sports scenes with precision—even treating the sports scenes as if he were getting ready for a real competitive game. Still, despite it being competitive, he was able to find a meditative, calm approach to understanding baseball that allowed him to keep his focus on the games (or rather, the scenes) while he was acting.

"You have to be calm, and you can't be inside your head," he said in a 2013 interview with The New York Times. "That's the beauty of what Jackie Robinson did—you take a sport where, if you're in your head, you make mistake

Rachel Robinson and Chadwick Boseman at the Los Angeles premiere of 42 on April 9, 2013, in Los Angeles. (Eric Charbonneau/Invision for Warner Bros./AP Images)

after mistake, and failing is what you do most of the time. Then you add all the other stuff going on around you, and you still manage to succeed? That's really what was amazing about it, and I didn't understand that until I was practicing it every day."

The film was released on April 23, 2013, and made about $97.5 million worldwide. The movie was met with generally good reviews, and critics began to notice how talented Chadwick Boseman really was. The review of the movie in *Entertainment Weekly* praised the actor, saying, "Boseman, a graceful and handsome actor with a deep inner fire, gives Robinson a stare that's penetrating and guarded at the same time. A lot of the film's drama is reading that face—the intelligence and masked outrage."

The Hollywood Reporter, in its review, went so far as to say that Boseman did a better job of playing Jackie Robinson than the actual Jackie Robinson himself; that is, better than

Chadwick Boseman exits the Brooklyn Dodgers team bus during filming of *42* at the Tutwiler Hotel, May 14, 2012, in Birmingham, Alabama. (AP Photo/The Birmingham News, Bernard Troncale)

Jackie Robinson's acting as himself in the 1950 movie *The Jackie Robinson Story*. Still, it's a tremendous compliment to give, and it was just one of many that Boseman would be receiving in his years to come as an actor in a lead role.

Bringing the Funk

Just a year after playing Jackie Robinson in *42*, Boseman was back at it again, ready to add the next big "great" to his acting résumé. This time, he would be going from the baseball field to the stage in bringing to life the one and only James Brown.

Though Boseman was the lead in the film, he was joined by a huge, star-studded cast for the 2014 movie. He acted alongside the likes of Dan Aykroyd, Viola Davis, Octavia Spencer, Craig Robinson, and Jill Scott, just to name a few.

This was yet another movie that not only took years to finally be made, but also originally had Spike Lee attached to the project. (It seems like 2020's *Da 5 Bloods* was finally a resolution in the Spike Lee–Boseman saga.) The movie's development dated back

Chadwick Boseman as James Brown in *Get on Up*. (Universal Pictures/Photofest)

to 2000 and was once titled *Superbad*. That was named after the 1970 James Brown song, of course, and pre-dated the 2007 movie *Superbad* starring Jonah Hill and Michael Cera. By 2006, the project fell apart, but it saw a second life in 2012.

Another barrier presented itself during the film's pre-production, and that barrier was Boseman himself. After playing Jackie Robinson in *42*, he wasn't quite ready to play another icon. And so he passed on the opportunity to play the lead role. Instead, he busied himself with some other projects, but director Tate Taylor wouldn't let Boseman abandon the film that easily.

And so, just months after the release of *42*, it was announced that Boseman had signed on to play James Brown in the biopic. By the time the film was released, Boseman was only thrusted further into the upper echelons of stardom.

"He's a hard worker and an artist," Octavia Spencer said to The Daily Beast in 2014. "The success of the film begins and ends with Chadwick's believability as James Brown, and he really pulls it off."

Time's review of the film compared Boseman's turn as the Godfather of Soul to Jamie Foxx's Oscar-winning performance as Ray Charles in *Ray*. Critic Richard Corliss boasted, "Incarnating James Brown in all his ornery uniqueness, he deserves a Pulitzer, a Nobel, and instant election to the Rock and Roll Hall of Fame."

While none of those came to fruition (not even an Oscar nomination), it was certain Boseman absolutely brought down the house when it came to this performance. But just how did he do it?

Jill Scott and Chadwick Boseman in *Get on Up*. (Universal Pictures/Photofest)

It takes a lot to feel the funk and bring the soul in only a way that James Brown could, and just like with *42*, it took a village to help Boseman find the soul within him. Yes, he did his own dance moves in the film, and he did *some* of the singing. But while Boseman looked absolutely flawless in the film, it wasn't necessarily like that during his rehearsals and training.

"During the test, we tried all the dances and I nailed none of them," Boseman said in the same Daily Beast interview. "My 'Mashed Potatoes' were uncooked, my 'Good Foot' was a bad foot, and my 'Get Up' was a fall-down. Everything was messed up. But it was good enough for me to see what it would be like to work with everybody, and I saw how crazy it was all going to look."

When it came to singing, the film was able to use live recordings of James Brown's when necessary. But Boseman still did his part to learn how to sing for the scenes that needed it. With his vocal coach, he basically undertook the training of an opera singer, singing at long intervals throughout the day to help refine his voice. The actor even got a few singing and performing tips from The Rolling Stones' Mick Jagger, who served as a producer on the film. The two would listen to recordings

Chadwick Boseman in *Get on Up*. (Universal Pictures/Photofest)

of Brown's concerts, and Jagger would point out the little things that Brown would do to signal the band or just give the audience the old razzle-dazzle.

To top it all off, Boseman met with Brown's family to piece together the entire picture, all of which led to one moving performance. The film opened on August 1, 2014. Making just slightly more than its $30 million budget at $33.4 million worldwide, the film still saw favorable reviews. Its only tragedy was that by the time awards season hit, it got little to no recognition when it came to the major awards, including radio silence from the Oscars and the Golden Globes.

Serving Justice

The offers just kept rolling in for Chadwick Boseman following his first two films as Jackie Robinson and James Brown. In 2015, already poised to play

Black Panther in *Captain America: Civil War*, it was announced that Boseman would be playing yet another influential person in American history: Supreme Court Justice Thurgood Marshall.

On choosing Thurgood Marshall to be the focus of his film, Reginald Hudlin said in a statement, "Thurgood Marshall was a man who took his life in his hands every time he came to a town to bring justice. Marshall was a cowboy who used his law books as guns. He was the smartest guy in the room of any room he was in. But he wasn't a punk and didn't hesitate to throw a punch if the occasion called for it."

That sounds like just the perfect person for Boseman to embody, and the announcement in December 2015 made it official. Surrounded by yet another star-studded cast, Boseman was proving himself to officially be a

Josh Gad and Chadwick Boseman in *Marshall*. (Open Road Films/Photofest)

part of Hollywood by that point. The film included stars Josh Gad, Kate Hudson, Dan Stevens, and even soon-to-be *Black Panther* co-star Sterling K. Brown.

Though Marshall is known for being the first Black judge to hold a seat on the Supreme Court, the film rewinds the clock back to one of Marshall's first cases as a lawyer. At an event at Compton High School in California, Boseman said of the movie, "First, I knew that this was not a story about Thurgood Marshall that people would know. You should know that he is a Supreme Court justice, but I knew people did not know this story—they did not know the ending of it."

Although this role wasn't as physically demanding for Boseman to play, the actor revealed that preparing for the part still involved a lot of physicality. So while there may not have been bases to steal or moves to learn, he did still have to learn how to physically embody Marshall in preparing for the role.

He told The Huffington Post in 2017, "There's a difference between the older man in the robes and the young, wiry version of Thurgood Marshall. I was coming off of *Captain America: Civil War*, so it was

Chadwick Boseman as Thurgood Marshall in *Marshall*. (Open Road Films/Photofest)

important that I didn't look like T'Challa in those suits. He couldn't look, like, super cut up in those suits. There's still the physicality of it, and there's still, to me, a sense of the physicality of the time period. It is the Harlem Renaissance and the jazz era, so although I didn't want to imitate what his voice might sound like or imitate his exact physicality, I did want to find the swagger or the rhythm of that time. So that is still very physical."

Through the story, Boseman also found a way to resonate with the character he was playing. Taking place during the Jim Crow era, Marshall was subject to hateful acts of discrimination. Boseman, growing up in the South, knew the effects that racism had in America firsthand. In a 2017 interview with NPR, he revealed, "I'm from Anderson, South Carolina, but I grew up in the South. So I know what it is to ride to school and have Confederate flags flying from trucks in front of me and behind me,

Thurgood Marshall Jr., Chadwick Boseman, Cecilia Marshall, and John Marshall attend the 21st Annual Urbanworld Film Festival at AMC Empire 25 theater on September 23, 2017, in New York City. (J. Countess/WireImage)

to see a parking lot full of people with Confederate flags and know what that means. I've been stopped by police for no reason. I've been called 'boy'...and everything else that you could imagine. Along with the great hospitality that is in the South, that is part of it."

The movie had a special early screening at Boseman's alma mater, Howard University, but the movie officially hit theaters on October 13, 2017. The film received mixed reviews, but most agreed that Boseman did the best he could with the material that he was given. IGN's review, for example, noted, "*Marshall* features some great performances, and might be worth watching just to see Chadwick Boseman alone."

For the *Chicago Sun-Times*, critic Richard Roeper wrote, "Boseman delivers perhaps his finest work to date—even when the material falters a

What Is the Jim Crow Era?

The Jim Crow era was a tense time in the 19th and 20th century United States when laws were put in place to justify racial segregation. This ranged from having separate entrances for Black people at public places to separating who could sit where on a bus. Although civil rights laws were enacted in the 1960s and progress has been made, the lasting effects of the Jim Crow era are still seen to this day.

bit and is more heavy-handed and pound-the-point-home than necessary... it's up to Boseman to carry the story, and that he does."

The film, with a budget of $12 million, grossed a little over $10 million worldwide. Luckily, a little-viewed movie was not going to stop Chadwick Boseman's career that easily. Because what he had lined up next was about to change his life forever. ♛

3

The Birth of a Hero

In 2014, the world was fully engrossed in superhero mania—specifically, Marvel mania. The company recently purchased by Disney was changing the world of cinema as fans knew it one movie at a time, building a network of complex and connected movies dating back to 2008's *Iron Man*. That movie sparked the beginning of the Marvel Cinematic Universe as we know it, and few could have guessed the Marvel machine would become as big as it is today.

In 2012, Marvel Studios reached a landmark when its first crossover movie, *The Avengers*, became a mega-hit. And within a few years' time, Marvel went from producing one movie a year, to two, to even three in the last few years. And smack-dab in the middle of that timeline was the introduction of Black Panther to the movie-viewing world.

Much like Steve Jobs' presentations that once created hype for the newest Apple creations each year, Marvel Studios president Kevin Feige

Chadwick Boseman promoting *Captain America: Civil War* at Univision Studios on September 12, 2016, in Miami. (John Parra/Getty Images)

took a stab at doing his own Apple-style presentation for Marvel Studios in October 2014. The event, held at the El Capitan Theatre in Los Angeles, was poised to introduce Phase 3 of the Marvel Cinematic Universe. All prior Marvel movies were grouped into two phases, the first beginning with *Iron Man* and the second concluding with *Ant Man*. With its future movies totally unknown up until that point, fans were anxious to see what the folks over at Marvel would be announcing for its next slate of movies. The audience in the theater was prepared for a spectacular event, and unlike a traditional comic convention (which typically don't stream panels, especially Marvel's), fans who couldn't make it in person got to watch the big announcements on their computers from any part of the globe.

The event was filled with announcements: the introduction of Captain Marvel and Doctor Strange, the newest Avengers movies, a sequel to the hit movie *Guardians of the Galaxy*, and, of course, the first ever Black Panther movie.

"T'Challa himself and all of Wakanda is one of the most unique, interesting, fascinating, and integral characters in the entire Marvel Comics history," Feige said following a thunderous round of applause when the movie was announced. "We want him to become that in the Marvel Cinematic Universe history. He's a bit of a prince, he may even become a bit of a king, but it's also about how this isolationist country of Wakanda needs to meet the world."

Later in the presentation, Robert Downey Jr. (Iron Man) and Chris Evans (Captain America) had the pleasure of

Robert Downey Jr., Chadwick Boseman, and Chris Evans onstage during Marvel Studios' fan event at the El Capitan Theatre on October 28, 2014, in Los Angeles. (Alberto E. Rodriguez/Getty Images for Disney)

announcing to the world that Chadwick Boseman would be taking the role of the Black Panther in the MCU. The crowd let out more roaring applause as Chadwick Boseman was announced on stage while the *Avengers* themed blasted behind him. There was a bonus announcement too: fans learned that Black Panther would be a key character in the newly announced *Captain America* sequel, *Captain America: Civil War*. So it wouldn't be too long before he was on screen.

When given the opportunity to say a few words to his co-stars, Boseman said, "I'm blessed to be a part of the Marvel universe and to work with you both. And I look forward to making magic together."

Little did Boseman know, the magic was going to be more than he could have ever imagined. The ecstatic fans were just getting a taste of what he was going to

Chadwick Boseman (as Black Panther), Paul Bettany (as Vision), Robert Downey Jr. (as Iron Man), Scarlett Johansson (as Black Widow), and Don Cheadle (as War Machine) in *Captain America: Civil War*. (Walt Disney Studios Motion Pictures/Photofest)

do for the MCU, and he hadn't even appeared in his first movie yet.

By the time 2016 rolled around, the year that *Captain America: Civil War* came out, the world was nothing but excited to see the Black Panther in his first film. And through various promotional tours for the monumental film, Boseman shared what it was like to be a real, on-screen superhero. Sure, the previous roles he played were heroes in a real-life sense, but putting on a suit and fighting bad guys was a whole different ballgame.

Luckily, Boseman felt welcomed in the MCU. Just as Black Panther was joining a team of superheroes in the movie world with the Avengers, Boseman in real life was joining the prestigious ranks of actors who appeared in the MCU.

During a set tour for the movie, Boseman said to the press, "I just think people have been very gracious and welcoming me on set, and even off set. What was more important was, you know, Chris [Evans] has been very cool in terms of inviting me to stuff and giving me a hard time in the best way. His sense of humor is great. Robert Downey has been great as well, [Anthony] Mackie—everybody. Everybody's been cool. Don Cheadle.

"So I've seen a lot of them separate from being here, so it didn't feel like when I got here it was like all of a sudden meeting them for the first time. I think that's what's weird, is when you step on the set and all of a sudden— you know, I've worked with really great actors before, but there's always a certain amount of nervous energy, just because you don't know these people."

Sebastian Stan and Chadwick Boseman attend a special screening of *Captain America: Civil War* at Brookfield Place, Henry R. Luce Auditorium, on May 4, 2016, in New York. (Evan Agostini/Invision/AP)

Nevertheless, Boseman shook off his nerves and gave the role his all. After all, Boseman made sure he was always prepared for the roles he played. Whether it was getting the physicality down or doing his research for the part, he was always on it. And with Black Panther, there came a bit of additional research he had to do that he hadn't done before, and that was brushing up on the comic books that would tell him everything he needed to know about his character.

In the same set tour, he said, "I think what you try to do is just get your hands on every single comic book you can find that has the character in it, or him being mentioned or anything. I've just tried to read them all—not like it's really work. It is work—don't get me wrong— it is work, but it's just sort of reading them like a kid, you know? Because when you just read it like it's work, you're just trying to get through it. So

I think it's putting yourself in that mind frame to go through the mythology in a fun way. And then, also, I've gone to South Africa, gone to some places, to see some things that I think relate to the character, and let those things sort of fuel your workouts, fuel your sessions when you work on the part."

And thus, after all his preparedness, Boseman proved that he was ready to be part of the next generation of superheroes. *Captain America: Civil War* released in theaters on May 6, 2016, and it was his biggest movie yet.

A Black Panther Summary of Captain America: Civil War

Unlike most silver-screen superheroes, Black Panther didn't get an origin story movie in the Marvel Cinematic Universe. Yes, *Black Panther* was a solo movie, but it jumps right into the action following T'Challa's story arc in *Captain America: Civil War*. While this movie

Promotional image for *Captain America:
Civil War*. (Marvel Studios/Photofest)

was mainly about Captain America (it was his sequel, after all), there were so many other superheroes involved that it contains two mini-origin stories: one for Spider-Man and one for Black Panther.

Black Panther's journey plays a large role in the overall story of *Civil War*, a movie in which Team Captain America and Team Iron Man face off when they reach a disagreement about the Avengers.

In the movie, a summit meeting of world leaders takes place at the United Nations headquarters in Vienna to discuss a disastrous event caused by the Avengers. In attendance is Natasha Romanoff (Black Widow), T'Challa of Wakanda, and his father, King T'Chaka of Wakanda. While T'Chaka is giving a speech, an explosion goes off, mortally wounding the king of Wakanda. T'Challa only has but a few moments to be with his father before he takes his last breath, and then T'Challa swears revenge on whoever caused the explosion that killed his father.

After following a false lead, T'Challa thinks Bucky Barnes (aka the Winter Soldier, Captain America's old friend) is the man who killed his father, and he picks a fight with the Winter Soldier despite his innocence. The real culprit was Helmut Zemo, who used the explosion to tear a deeper rift between the Avengers by framing Bucky. At one point, the Avengers are so caught up in their own drama and distracted from what's really going on that they have an epic showdown at an airport, and that's when the real civil war begins between Iron Man's allies and Captain America's.

T'Challa (who assumed the mantle of the Black Panther from his father) joined the fight on Iron Man's side to stop the Winter Soldier once and for all. Bucky escaped the battle, but it didn't mean T'Challa was done hunting him down.

Captain America, Iron Man, and the Winter Soldier later had a confrontation with Zemo present, and the villain made a getaway while the heroes fought one another. We learned his plan for tearing the Avengers apart was

Chadwick Boseman as T'Challa in *Captain America: Civil War*. (Marvel Studios/Photofest)

because he lost his family due to the Avengers' destruction of his hometown. With Zemo set on taking his own life after finally exacting his revenge, Black Panther finds him just in time to stop him and take him to the authorities.

After having a change of heart about seeking revenge, Black Panther was eventually able to accept the Winter Soldier's innocence. And he even agreed to keep the hero (who was now an outlaw) safe in his hidden home country of Wakanda. The death of his father all led up to the story of his coronation in *Black Panther*, and his allyship with Bucky Barnes would eventually play a larger role in *Avengers: Infinity War*, where Wakanda became the setting for the final battle.

The Panther Reigns King

After the opening weekend, the results were in; anyone could have predicted it. *Captain America: Civil War* was the No. 1 movie in America. The film,

directed by brothers Joe and Anthony Russo, surpassed expectations; it grossed about $1.1 billion worldwide, making it one of the top five highest-grossing Marvel movies at that time.

Boseman had entered the cinematic universe at a time when Marvel Studios was crossing a threshold: all of its movies were beginning to not only reach the $1 billion mark at the box office, but more often than not surpass it. Fans were turning out in droves to see these movies. More people were heading out to theaters to see it, and more people were watching the movies multiple times in theaters.

That was the precedent set for *Black Panther*. And that's what made the post-credits scene in *Captain America: Civil War* so special. By dropping those little breadcrumbs about the Black Panther harboring the Winter Soldier in his country and giving fans the slightest glimpse of Wakanda, it drove up anticipation even more for the solo movie.

Speaking to POPSUGAR in 2016 following the movie's release, Boseman teased how excited he was about the *Captain America* sequel's end-credits scene. He said, "[The scene] made me feel confident. They've been saying they were gonna do it and my purpose of this movie—part of it—was to further the storyline they already had. It felt like Black Panther was a strong character to do that third storyline, but it was also to introduce the character and make people be ready. The fact that they did that let me know that they thought he was strong enough."

The stage was now set for Chadwick Boseman to take control in his own movie. He played nicely with the Avengers, but there was so much more to discover in his upcoming solo movie—which, at that time, was

Stay Until the Very End

Marvel has become a master at writing mid-credits and post-credits scenes. These scenes tend to tease the next movie set to come out in the Marvel Cinematic Universe, or they're used to throw one last joke into the movie you just watched. While it's a good tool to get fans hyped about the next film, it also encourages audiences to watch the credits all the way through and see the names of the hardworking people who made the film possible.

still roughly two years away from hitting theaters. During that time, Marvel dropped more of its Phase 3 movies, including *Doctor Strange* and *Thor: Ragnarok*. And while those movies had their own passionate fanbases and followings, nothing could prepare Marvel for the behemoth of a phenomenon that *Black Panther* was going to bring in February 2018.

The History of Black Panther

Now you know the backstory behind Black Panther's inception in the Marvel Cinematic Universe. But do you know the history of Black Panther in the comic books? It's one that even Chadwick Boseman himself got to study as he learned more about Black history at Howard University. And in his research for the role, he learned even more about the hero, his comic-book origins, and even current runs of the comic-book character.

The birth of Black Panther starts with Marvel Comics' most iconic figure: Stan Lee. Many credit Stan Lee for his creation of some of Marvel's most famous characters, but few also know that it was writer and artist Jack Kirby who was behind some of those characters' classic designs as well. The two created the likes of Iron Man, Thor, the Hulk, the Fantastic Four, the X-Men, and many more, so it's no wonder Black Panther would soon become an iconic hero as well thanks to their help.

The character originally didn't get his own comic-book run. He first appeared in *Fantastic Four #52* and *#53* when they were released in 1966. And it must be noted that Black Panther was the first Black superhero to appear in a major comic-book series. Yes, among other Black superheroes like Marvel's Luke Cage, Blade, and the Falcon, Black Panther was first. He even came before the likes of DC's

John Stewart/Green Lantern and Black Lightning.

The reasoning behind Black Panther's creation was simple. It was as if a lightbulb went off in Stan Lee's head one day: comic books needed Black superheroes. He had Black friends who were creators just as he was, but they had no characters who looked like them. It was a simple question of "Why not?" that changed the game for the comic-book industry. And no, Stan Lee said the name "Black Panther" has no relation to the Black Panther Party, which came after T'Challa's debut. But Black Panther did temporarily receive a name change to Black Leopard in the 1970s to avoid confusion, but that didn't work out so well.

And so, the story of T'Challa was born. The African king from the fictional country of Wakanda, a high-tech nation that advanced because of its mysterious, exclusive resource: vibranium. The element is in his suit; it's in his claws; it's everywhere! (Some may recognize that even Captain America's shield is made out of vibranium.) In his early years, Black Panther quickly joined the Avengers. And by 1977, he finally got his own series (which Jack Kirby took the lead on), and that set the tone for the many adventures Black Panther would have in the future. Some of his most notable story arcs have included his marriage to the X-Men's Storm and joining Captain America in the Civil War arc. But luckily, if you're not caught up on the comics, *Black Panther* the movie did quite a good job of adapting the T'Challa that fans have known on the page for decades.

Wakanda Forever

The moment had finally come. Marvel would be putting out its first-ever solo movie starring a Black superhero. Not only that—an African superhero. This was largely unprecedented. And Chadwick Boseman would be at the forefront of that moment.

Boseman, though, wasn't the first Black superhero in film history, nor was he the first Black superhero in Marvel Studios' history. Nick Fury, played by Samuel L. Jackson, was one of the first leading characters to play a major role in the Marvel Cinematic Universe—though his character isn't necessarily considered a superhero in this franchise. In 2008's *Iron Man*, Terrence Howard played Colonel James Rhodes, friend to Iron Man, but he never got the chance to be a superhero. Howard was later replaced by Don Cheadle, who became Iron Man's partner in crimefighting, War Machine. Later,

Chadwick Boseman in *Black Panther*. (Walt Disney Studios Motion Pictures/Photofest)

Anthony Mackie joined the MCU as the Falcon, friend to Captain America.

But there was a trend here. Yes, there were Black superheroes in the MCU, but mostly all of them seemed to play second fiddle to their white counterpart. *Doctor Strange* fell into this pattern, when Chiwetel Ejiofor played the side character Karl Mordo. Idris Elba played a side character in the *Thor* movies as Heimdall. The list went on. Yes, those characters played significant roles, but they were usually the sidekick and never the star of the show. *Black Panther* was different because Black Panther was no sidekick.

That in and of itself was worth celebrating, especially for the Black fans who were thrilled to see this kind of representation on screen. And the movie came right at a time when discussions about diversity and representation were becoming more and more prominent. For a long time, Hollywood seemed fixated on the myth that "Black movies" didn't sell, or that no one would want to

Director Ryan Coogler and Chadwick Boseman on the set of *Black Panther*. (Walt Disney Studios Motion Pictures/Photofest)

see a movie with a Black character in the lead. Even as film studios began to (slowly) increase the number of movies with Black leads, movies with white leads and majority-white casts largely outnumbered any of those other movies. This stereotyping has an unfortunate and detrimental effect, and there were far and few instances where people of color could point to a hero in a movie and connect with that individual.

So, for Chadwick Boseman to be the lead role as a Black superhero was absolutely groundbreaking. Now, people of all ages had the chance to see their culture, their skin color, and their lives represented on screen in Hollywood's biggest blockbuster franchise. Not only that, but the world at large would get to experience the rich culture of Africa, far from any tragic depictions from movies of the past.

In *Black Panther*, you saw not just an African man, but a king. A protector of his people and a land more advanced than anywhere else on the globe.

Marvel understood that a film about a Black nation would benefit from a Black director. Ryan Coogler helmed the movie after directing just two feature films (*Fruitvale Station* and *Creed*). Both films starred Michael B. Jordan, and Coogler brought the actor with him into the cast of this film. Coogler also sought out actors of African descent, including Oscar-winning actress Lupita Nyong'o (who is part Kenyan) and Danai Gurira (whose parents are Zimbabwean). He rounded out the cast with a handful of other actors including Letitia Wright, Daniel Kaluuya, Winston Duke, Sterling K. Brown, Andy Serkis, Martin Freeman, and acting legends Angela Bassett and Forest Whitaker.

Chadwick Boseman as T'Challa in *Black Panther*. (Walt Disney Studios Motion Pictures/Photofest)

In addition, Coogler and his team made sure that they did all the research they could to do justice to a story about an African hero. In preparation, Coogler made sure he traveled to Africa to gather inspiration for his film. He told NPR in 2018, "For me, it was about this question of 'What does it mean to be African?' It was a question I couldn't answer. When I was taking this project, it was a question I needed to answer about myself, you know, which is the personal connection that I'm talking about. And it's a question that sounds specific, but it's actually universal for a lot of reasons.... I mean if you ask yourself, 'Now what does it mean to be Ukrainian?' or 'What does it mean to be Eurasian?' It's a deep question, right, if you think about it. It's not a question you can answer with one word. But it's a question you can spend your life trying to figure out, and have fun doing it, I truly believe."

On Boseman's end, another part of that preparation came from discovering his own African ancestry. "One of the key factors was me getting a sense of my background," he told *Variety* in 2018. And so, Boseman took a DNA test to discover his African roots and found out the specific ethnic groups his families came from, including groups from Nigeria and Sierra Leone.

In the creation of the character, Boseman even pushed Marvel to let T'Challa have an African accent. That, to him, was very important, despite the worrying of some executives. Still, he persisted, telling *The Hollywood Reporter*, "They felt that it was maybe too much for an audience to take. I felt the exact opposite—like, if I speak with a British accent, what's gonna happen when I go home?

"It felt to me like a deal-breaker. I was like, 'No, this is such an important factor

Chadwick Boseman in *Black Panther*. (Walt Disney Studios Motion Pictures/Photofest)

that if we lose this right now, what else are we gonna throw away for the sake of making people feel comfortable?'"

That was just one of the small yet meaningful victories for representation when it came to *Black Panther*. The creators formed a Wakandan language that characters spoke, which was based on Xhosa, one of the official languages of South Africa. Boseman even got a personal lesson from his own father— well, his on-screen father. South African actor John Kani, who plays T'Chaka in the MCU, spoke Xhosa and was able to teach some to Boseman on set.

The pieces for production were in place. Fans were bursting at the seams to see the new movie. Tickets were being bought well in advance, and cosplayers were preparing to wear their best *Black Panther*-inspired costumes. Even people who didn't typically cosplay were ready to dress up for the occasion, donning their best African garb to celebrate and even buying African-inspired outfits if they didn't already have them at home.

That, in a nutshell, is essentially what *Black Panther* became: a celebration. The movie came out on February 16, 2018, right in the middle of Black History Month. And that certainly made it even more of a momentous occasion for fans eager to see their hero on screen. People were sharing on social media what they would wear to the premiere, talked about how many times they were going to see it, and, in general, kept the momentum alive for the movie's debut. And it was moviegoers' passionate support for the film that proved to be a gamechanger not just for Marvel Studios, but for Hollywood as a whole.

Author Ta-Nehisi Coates with *Black Panther* stars Chadwick Boseman and Lupita Nyong'o at the Apollo Theater on February 27, 2018, in New York City. (Shahar Azran/WireImage)

More Than a Hero, More Than a Movie

Scroll back to any social media feed during February 2018, and all you'll find is evidence of how much of a success *Black Panther* was. The first Marvel Studios film to be directed by a Black director and to have a majority Black cast shattered records on its first weekend. Making just over $201 million, it became the fifth-biggest movie opening of all time. The movie also topped 2016's *Deadpool*, based on another Marvel character, to become the largest grossing movie ever released in February.

Just as the Marvel model had created with its past movies, people who didn't even consider themselves superhero fans were beginning to show up and see the movie. And so many went to see the movie multiple times. They

Chadwick Boseman in *Black Panther.* (Walt Disney Studios Motion Pictures/Photofest)

Box-Office King

Did you know Chadwick Boseman appeared in three of the top-grossing movies of all time? As of this publishing, *Black Panther* is currently the 12th-highest-grossing movie in history, making over $1.3 billion at the box office. At No. 5 is 2018's *Avengers: Infinity War*, which brought in over $2 billion worldwide. And last but not least, Chadwick Boseman starred in the highest-grossing movie ever: *Avengers: Endgame*. The 2019 film made over $2.7 billion worldwide, beating the previous records once held by James Cameron's *Titanic* (1997) and *Avatar* (2009).

March 19, the movie continued to play in theaters well throughout the summer box-office season. At one point in 2018, Marvel had three of its movies in theaters at once. *Avengers: Infinity War* (the highest-grossing movie of the year) was released in April. *Captain Marvel* was released in March. And, with *Black Panther's* help, the three new Marvel movies ran side by side in theaters—something never seen before in movie history.

Eventually, the movie topped the box-office charts, making over $1.3 billion worldwide in its run; as of 2020, *Black Panther* is the 12th-highest-grossing movie of all time.

would go see it, and then they'd tell a friend to come see it with them again, and then they'd bring more people to see it, and the cycle went on for weeks.

While Box Office Mojo lists *Black Panther's* original run as ending on

But it wasn't just about the money. The long-lasting effects that *Black Panther* had was the biggest takeaway for most fans. Of all the monumental things *Black Panther* had done, part of it was helping Black viewers connect

Poster art for *Black Panther*. (Walt Disney Studios Motion Pictures/Photofest)

to their roots and their history, one that was rarely ever taught to them in history books. And they finally had the opportunity to celebrate that past.

Speaking to Trevor Noah on *The Daily Show with Trevor Noah*, Boseman agreed with the host that the movie bridged the gap between African people and Black America's perception of the continent.

"I can't even begin to put in words what that feels like because on both sides, as an African American and seeing people from the continent, I've seen a divide my entire life," Boseman told Noah. "And then I went through my phase of trying to find Africa and not knowing, 'Well, which place was I from?' And I've seen Africans who viewed us in a particular way where, 'You're not connected. You don't know where you're from.' And at the same time, loving parts of our culture… So this movie, in a certain way, creates a story that we all share. And it's the first time I feel like that's ever happened where it feels like: 'That's our story,' 'That's our story too.'"

The rallying cry for Wakanda is the famous "Wakanda forever!" For those who perhaps didn't know their African ancestry and those who celebrated the movie, Wakanda gave them a sense of home. Though fictional, they could claim Wakanda as their own, if only to anchor their journey in learning about their heritage and their roots. Boseman was just the same, seeing as he was led on a discovery of his roots when he joined the movie. And the embrace of this culture opened the doors for people to want more. More Black and African history. More Black and African writers, directors, actors, designers. The possibilities were endless. Just like Wakanda, no longer would the culture be sidelined or hidden from plain sight.

The doors were wide open to connecting all people to the motherland. And like T'Challa's message at the end of *Black Panther*, the movie made it certain that we shouldn't be divided. We must all look after one another "as if we were one single tribe."

Michael B. Jordan, Letitia Wright, Chadwick Boseman, Lupita Nyong'o, Daniel Kaluuya, and Danai Gurira at the premiere of *Black Panther* on February 8, 2018, in London, England. (Joel C Ryan/Invision/AP)

Black Panther Characters

T'Challa/Black Panther: T'Challa is the new king of Wakanda. Inheriting the throne from his late father, T'Challa's goal is to learn what it takes to be a king and how to be an even better one than his father.

Erik "Killmonger" Stevens: The American cousin of T'Challa, Killmonger is set on becoming the king of Wakanda after watching his people suffer while Wakanda turned a blind eye.

Shuri: The younger sister of T'Challa, Shuri is the science nerd of the family, coming up with all kinds of vibranium-infused inventions to advance their nation—including the Panther suit.

T'Chaka: The former Black Panther, T'Chaka was the father of T'Challa. He killed his brother (Killmonger's father) after discovering his wrongdoings in America.

Ramonda: Ramonda is the queen of Wakanda, widow to T'Chaka and the mother to Shuri and T'Challa. She makes sure her children keep their heads on their shoulders and always offers them support.

Nakia: An excellent spy for Wakanda, Nakia is the long-time friend of T'Challa who helps him in his battles and eventually becomes his love interest.

Okoye: Okoye is the captain of the Dora Milaje, the all-women warrior team that protects the king, no matter what.

M'Baku: A challenger to the throne of Wakanda, M'Baku comes from the Wakandan Jabari tribe, people who seek to live more traditionally than those in the city.

From the set of *Black Panther*: Michael B. Jordan as Erik "Killmonger" Stevens and Chadwick Boseman as T'Challa. (Walt Disney Studios Motion Pictures/ Photofest)

W'Kabi: W'Kabi is the leader of the warriors of the Wakandan Border Tribe and he's the husband to Okoye. He switches his allegiance to Killmonger after disagreeing with T'Challa's reign.

Ulysses Klaue: The evil mastermind known as Klaue is bent on making a fortune by smuggling vibranium and vibranium weapons out of Wakanda. He enlists Killmonger's help to do so.

N'Jobu: Father of Killmonger and the brother of T'Chaka, N'Jobu was a traitor to Wakanda who secretly helped Klaue smuggle vibranium out of Wakanda in the '90s.

Everett Ross: An American agent, Ross is put on Klaue's case and teams up with Black Panther to help stop him.

Zuri: Thought by N'Jobu to be an American friend named James, Zuri is a Wakandan posing as an American by the king's orders to spy on N'Jobu.

(top) Lupita Nyong'o as Nakia, Boseman, and Danai Gurira as Okoye; (right) Nyong'o, Boseman, and Letitia Wright as Shuri. (Walt Disney Studios Motion Pictures/Photofest)

5

Making Oscars History

To star in a movie is one accomplishment. To star in an Oscar-nominated movie is a different success all on its own. And by January 2019, Chadwick Boseman and the cast and crew of *Black Panther* could proudly declare that they were part of an Oscar-nominated movie. And no, the movie hadn't just been nominated for one Oscar. This time, it was all about lucky number seven. Yes, *Black Panther* had received a total of seven Oscar nominations, including one for the biggest prize of the night: Best Picture.

In just a few short years, Boseman had gone from acting in small parts on TV to being the lead in a Best Picture–nominated movie. And, for him, this was one of the most promising awards seasons in all of his career. Prior to *Black Panther*, there was barely any recognition from major awards shows when it came to his work. Looking back on the big three biopics (*42, Get on Up*, and *Marshall*), *Marshall* was the only film to be nominated for an Academy Award. And even then, the award was for Original Song ("Stand Up for Something" by Common and Diane Warren). *Get on Up* was nominated for a Screen Actors Guild Award in 2015, but even that nomination was only for the best stunt ensemble.

Many could think that his work in all three of those movies was worthy of an Oscar, especially given the immense amount of effort he put into playing the roles. But luckily, *Black Panther* came along to capture the zeitgeist and bring Boseman and the crew a fantastic awards season.

At the Academy Awards, *Black Panther* was nominated for Best Picture, Best Original Score, Best Original Song, Best Costume Design, Best Production Design, Best Sound Editing, and Best Sound Mixing.

Chadwick Boseman poses with the award for outstanding actor in a motion picture for *Black Panther* at the 50th annual NAACP Image Awards on March 30, 2019, at the Dolby Theatre in Los Angeles. (Richard Shotwell/Invision/AP)

On social media, actress Lupita Nyong'o shared her reaction to the nominations with a clip of her at San Diego Comic-Con in 2017 with Boseman and others. In the caption, she wrote:

Lupita Nyong'o✓
@Lupita_Nyongo

Seven #OscarNoms for #BlackPanther, including best picture!! This is our reaction the first time we saw footage from the film and we're feeling this way all over again today! Thank you @TheAcademy! #WakandaForever #Oscars

9:18 AM • Jan. 22, 2019

Actress Letitia Wright, who plays Shuri, responded to the news by sharing:

Letitia Wright✓
@letitiawright

History was made again this morning. 7 #OscarNominations including Best Picture! God is truly amazing.

Thank you all for the love and support. Honestly we made this movie out of love and wanted to inspire the world with it.

Thank you!

@TheAcademy @theblackpanther #Oscars

11:24 AM • Jan. 22, 2019

Director Ryan Coogler was, of course, extremely happy to see his film receiving such high recognition. He told *Entertainment Tonight* in an interview, "I think, for us, we were just trying to make a movie as best as we could. And to have it embraced, like it has been, has been incredible. And for people to still be thinking about it and talking about it, especially a year after it came out, it's a deep honor, man. And it doesn't always happen. So I just feel fortunate."

With all the good news from the Oscars buzz, it was unfortunate to see that neither the cast nor Coogler were nominated in any other major categories. Unlike many Best Picture movies, *Black Panther* didn't get an accompanying Best Actor nomination to go with it, meaning Boseman wasn't nominated for an acting award at the Oscars—nor was the rest of the cast.

The cast of *Black Panther* accepts the award for outstanding performance by a cast in a motion picture at the 25th annual Screen Actors Guild Awards at the Shrine Auditorium & Expo Hall on January 27, 2019, in Los Angeles. (Richard Shotwell/Invision/AP)

But to make up for that, the cast received a huge nomination from the Screen Actors Guild for Outstanding Performance by a Cast. While the SAG Awards usually aren't as popular as the Oscars or even the Golden Globes, this year was an exception because the *Black Panther* cast got justice by being nominated in the category. The list of actors included Boseman, Michael B. Jordan, Lupita Nyong'o, Letitia Wright, Danai Gurira, Angela Bassett, Forest Whitaker, Winston Duke, Sterling K. Brown, Daniel Kaluuya, Martin Freeman, and Andy Serkis. Additionally, an even longer list (approximately 201 names) were nominated for Best Stunt Ensemble, so the talented performers who brought *Black Panther* to the screen were certainly acknowledged at the SAG Awards.

On top of all that, *Black Panther* received recognition from the Golden Globes as well. Nominated for Best Drama Picture, Best Original Score, and Best Original Song, things were certainly shaping up to be an exciting awards season.

On January 27, 2019, the *Black Panther* cast celebrated their win at the SAG Awards. As the movie's name was called, the actors jumped up for joy, hugging one another with huge smiles on their faces. Boseman gave Michael B. Jordan a congratulatory hug, and the cast made their way to the stage to accept their award amidst a standing ovation from the entire celebrity-filled room. Angela Bassett accepted the green award statuette, but it was Chadwick Boseman who stood at the microphone to deliver one of his most inspiring speeches yet:

This cast, this ensemble. When I think of going to work every day and the passion

Chadwick Boseman and wife Taylor Simone Ledward arrive at the 25th annual Screen Actors Guild Awards at the Shrine Auditorium & Expo Hall on January 27, 2019, in Los Angeles. (Matt Sayles/Invision/AP)

and the intelligence, the resolve, the discipline that everybody showed, I also think of two questions that we all have received during the course of multiple publicity runs. And one is, "Did we know that this movie was going to receive this kind of response?" Meaning, was it going to make a billion dollars, was it going to still be around during award season? And the second question is, "Has it changed the industry?" Has it actually changed the way this industry works, how it sees us?

And my answer is to be young, gifted, and Black... Because all of us up here, and Andy [Serkis], we include you, too... To be young, gifted, and Black, we all know what it's like to be told that there is not a place for you to be featured, yet you are young, gifted, and Black.

We know what it's like to be told there's not a screen for you to be featured on, a stage for you to be featured on. We

know what it's like to be the tail and not the head. We know what it's like to be beneath and not above. And that is what we went to work with every day because we knew—not that we would be around during award season or that it would make a billion dollars—but we knew we had something special that we wanted to give the world. That we could be full human beings in the roles that we were playing, that we could create a world that exemplified a world that we wanted to see.

We knew that we had something that we wanted to give. And to come to work every day and to solve problems with this group of people every day, with this director, that is something that I wish all actors would get the opportunity to experience. If you get to experience that, you will be a fulfilled artist.

Now, the question of, you know, will we be around?... The question of will we be *around during award season, I just have to say, it's a pleasure to be celebrated by you, to be loved by you. And one thing I do know: did it change the industry? I know that you can't have a Black Panther now without a 2 on it. So, we love you. And we celebrate it.*

The crux of Boseman's speech that night, "To be young, gifted, and Black," came from the Nina Simone song of the

Chadwick Boseman, Danai Gurira, Lupita Nyong'o, and Michael B. Jordan strike a familiar pose onstage during the 76th annual Golden Globe Awards at the Beverly Hilton Hotel on January 6, 2019, in Beverly Hills, California. (Paul Drinkwater/NBCUniversal via Getty Images)

same name. In the song, Simone sings: "In the whole world you know there's a million boys and girls who are young, gifted, and Black. And that's a fact. You are young, gifted, and Black. We must begin to tell our young there's a world waiting for you. Yours is a quest that's just begun."

Nearly 50 years after the song was released, the lyrics were still resonating with this generation of young Black people. Like Boseman said, for them, the phenomenon wasn't about breaking box-office records, it was about giving back to a community and opening doors for others. By sharing their talents and creating something never seen before, they would be setting the curve for the future: a future where aspiring Black actors could get their dream role, or direct a feature film, or even win an Oscar for their work.

Black Panther continued winning during awards season, racking up victories from numerous bodies, including the American Film Institute, the Critics' Choice Movie Awards, and the People's Choice Awards. Boseman also won the Outstanding Actor award at the NAACP Image Awards, and *Black Panther* was named Movie of the Year at the MTV Movie & TV Awards.

On Oscars night 2019, the anticipation was high as all eyes were on *Black Panther*. It would be a revolutionary win if it became the first superhero film in Oscars history to win Best Picture. Everyone knows the Oscars favor period dramas and biopics, but this would be a game-changer. At the following year's ceremony, the Oscars even nominated the comic book–based movie *Joker* for multiple awards,

Winston Duke, Chadwick Boseman, and Michael B. Jordan accept the award for best movie for *Black Panther* at the MTV Movie & TV Awards at the Barker Hangar on June 16, 2018, in Santa Monica, California. (Matt Sayles/Invision/AP)

so it seemed like the Academy was changing its view on the genre.

As the night progressed, *Black Panther* began slowly but surely to collect a few wins from its seven nominations. It was Ruth E. Carter's win for Best Costume Design that won Marvel its first Oscar ever. Then, *Black Panther*'s Hannah Beachler brought in the next award for Production Design. But they weren't just making Marvel history. They were making Oscars history. Carter was the first Black woman to win Best Costume Design. And Beachler was the first Black person to win Best Production Design—not only that, but she was the first Black person ever to be nominated for the award. After accepting her award, Beachler was backstage and said, "There was never any doubt in my mind that I wanted to do the film because I knew what Ryan [Coogler] would do with it and what it would become—not just a superhero film, but a film for the ages."

Composer Ludwig Göransson also nabbed the Oscar for Best Original Score. That brought the grand total of Oscars up to three for *Black Panther*, but that would be the final total. By the end of the night, when Best Picture was announced, the winner for the 91st Academy Awards' Best Picture went to *Green Book,* the film starring Viggo Mortensen and Mahershala Ali.

The loss of the big award may have been a disappointing moment for some. But the loss shouldn't be overshadowed by just how big *Black Panther*'s nomination was in the first place. Chadwick Boseman, Ryan Coogler, and the rest of the crew involved in *Black Panther* set a new precedent for movies in Hollywood, as studios became more accepting of diverse movies from a variety of genres. Especially following the #OscarsSoWhite Movement that put the spotlight on the Oscars to nominate more people of color, it was becoming clear that change and progress was being made. And with Chadwick Boseman and *Black Panther* at the center of that, there's still hope today that many more actors and creatives will follow in those footsteps.

Lady Gaga and Chadwick Boseman backstage during the 91st annual Academy Awards at the Dolby Theatre on February 24, 2019, in Hollywood, California. (Matt Petit/A.M.P.A.S. via Getty Images)

Chadwick Boseman arrives at the 91st annual Academy Awards at Hollywood and Highland on February 24, 2019, in Hollywood, California. (Steve Granitz/WireImage)

A Brief Oscars Black History Timeline

1940: Hattie McDaniel becomes the first African American person to win an Oscar, for *Gone with the Wind*.

1964: Sidney Poitier becomes the first Black person to win Best Actor.

1972: Isaac Hayes becomes first Black person to win Best Original Song.

1983: Louis Gossett Jr. is the first Black person to win Best Supporting Actor.

1985: Stevie Wonder wins Best Original Song.

1985: Prince wins Best Original Song Score for *Purple Rain*.

1990: Denzel Washington wins Best Supporting Actor for *Glory*.

1991: Whoopi Goldberg is the second Black actress to win Best Supporting Actress.

2002: Halle Berry becomes the first Black woman to win Best Actress, in *Monster's Ball*.

2005: Morgan Freeman wins Best Supporting Actor for *Million Dollar Baby*.

2005: Jamie Foxx wins Best Actor for *Ray*.

2006: Three 6 Mafia are the first rappers to win an Oscar.

2007: Forest Whitaker wins Best Actor for *The Last King of Scotland*.

2007: Jennifer Hudson wins Best Supporting Actress for *Dreamgirls*.

2010: Geoffrey Fletcher is the first Black person to win Best Adapted Screenplay for *Precious*.

2012: Octavia Spencer wins Best Supporting Actress for *The Help*.

2014: Lupita Nyong'o wins Best Supporting Actress for *12 Years a Slave*.

2017: Mahershala Ali wins Best Supporting Actor for *Moonlight*, becoming the first Muslim actor to win an Oscar.

2018: Jordan Peele's *Get Out* win makes him the first Black person to win Best Original Screenplay.

2019: Ruth E. Carter becomes first Black winner for Costume Design and Hannah Beachler is the first Black winner for Production Design, for *Black Panther*.

2020: Matthew A. Cherry's *Hair Love* wins Best Animated Short.

A Man
of Heart

Chapter 6: A Man of Heart

Being a part of *Black Panther*, Chadwick Boseman stepped into a film that was full of love and unity both on screen and off. The movie held a powerful message about family. How do you love and support your loved ones through thick and thin? In the film, even as Killmonger lay dying, Black Panther put aside their differences and held him in his arms as they watched the sun set beautifully over Wakanda. And what of your acquaintances, even if they are rivals? Midway through the film, M'Baku (who opposed Black Panther for the throne) housed the dying king—no questions asked—to ensure he was well looked after.

The prevailing sense that love and unity conquer all was absolutely rampant in *Black Panther*, among its many other messages. But that sense of coming together, showing compassion and helping one another as if we were one tribe, was taking place well before the movie began playing in theaters. One man had an idea to help a local group of children see *Black Panther* for free, and within weeks, it ended up becoming a worldwide phenomenon.

It was called the Black Panther Challenge. And it was started by a young professional by the name of Frederick Joseph. The original goal for Joseph was to start a GoFundMe campaign to let kids in Harlem, New York, see the film for free. He found the idea of diversity and representation extremely important for children, especially after a viewing of Pixar's *Coco*. And thus, he launched the campaign for the Harlem Boys & Girls Club.

Through social media, the campaign began to pick up notoriety, and it was taking the Internet by storm. People like Snoop Dogg and Ellen DeGeneres

Chadwick Boseman attends the Global Charity Initiative Benefit at the Beverly Hilton Hotel on October 27, 2019, in Beverly Hills, California. (Paul Archuleta/Getty Images)

were among the first celebrities to begin sharing the campaign. Soon, Joseph had raised over $40,000. After surpassing his goal, he encouraged others to begin campaigns for children in other areas to see *Black Panther*. Pretty soon, hundreds of GoFundMe campaigns were created for #TheBlackPantherChallenge so children could see the movie for free.

In late January 2018, Ellen DeGeneres even invited Joseph to a taping of her show on the day that Chadwick Boseman would be a guest. After his interview, DeGeneres surprised Joseph by inviting him on stage so he could meet Boseman personally and tell him his story.

GoFundMe reported that in the time the campaign launched and was active, over 600 affiliated campaigns were created across the United States and in 50 countries around the world. This meant kids from Baltimore to Berlin would have

the chance to see the movie thanks to the generous efforts of the public.

One video of children learning they would get to see *Black Panther* went viral. At the Ron Clark Academy in Atlanta, the kids broke out in dance to celebrate the news. The clip was even shown to Boseman that February when he appeared on *The View*. Boseman admitted he had seen the viral video previously, and when asked what seeing the kids' reaction meant to him, he told the hosts, "That's why you do this. That's the reason why, for me, it's one of the reasons why I get up in the morning and I do what I do. Like, there's actually a couple of kids that I've connected with while I was shooting *Black Panther* and literally when I was tired, I just think of them, you know? So, thinking about them seeing [the] movie. And so to see that, it means that much. You know, sometimes you can psych yourself out and believe

Chadwick Boseman and *42* co-star Nicole Beharie attend the Jackie Robinson Foundation Awards Gala at the Waldorf-Astoria on March 5, 2012, in New York City. (Stephen Lovekin/Getty Images for The Jackie Robinson Foundation)

that what you're doing is more important than you think it is. But it's obviously not the case."

In a statement regarding the campaign, Frederick Joseph said, "All children deserve to believe they can save the world, go on exciting adventures, or accomplish the impossible. I am grateful that all of you have answered the call and are taking action to help more kids watch their heroes on the big screen."

By the time the campaign ended, the 600 GoFundMe campaigns amassed nearly $1 million in funds. It marked a small turning point for the world to come together amid all the chaos and noise of daily life. Undoubtedly, not only was *Black Panther* an opportunity to celebrate, but it was also a time to give back, to educate, and to just be reminded of the goodness in people's hearts. Surely, out of all the children

who got the chance to see Boseman on screen, there were some who were inspired—inspired by T'Challa to be like a king or inspired by Shuri to be a tech wiz. Or, some may have even seen the kindness in the act, and they may be inspired to give back to future generations the same way they were helped that day.

A Beacon of Light

Though Boseman wasn't the founder of the Black Panther Challenge, he found his own ways to give back to deserving communities in need. And without a doubt, he was certainly there for his fans by and by. But it wasn't until after his death that most people began to realize how much of a charitable person Boseman really was.

In his spare time, Boseman was working with the Make-A-Wish-Foundation to help children with cancer. It was an incredibly

Chadwick Boseman speaks onstage during the Los Angeles Dodgers Foundation Inaugural Blue Diamond Gala at Dodger Stadium on April 16, 2015, in Los Angeles. (Allen Berezovsky/WireImage)

selfless thing to do, and fans were amazed to learn that during his numerous hospital visits to see children, he was also battling his own struggle at the same time. One young fan wrote a blog on the St. Jude Children's Research Hospital website about her experience meeting Boseman. The young woman was undergoing treatment for a brain tumor, and in 2018, she attended a special *Black Panther* screening organized by St. Jude. Little did she and the kids know, Boseman would be dropping in on their party to pay them a visit.

She wrote on the blog: "When I walked up to him with my sister… he said he liked our face painting. I told him the pink lines were painted to honor the tribal marks our dad, who is from Nigeria, has on his face. He was truly interested and asked me where our dad was from and what tribe. His genuine interest in talking to me, that's what struck me when I first met him."

You could tell that his work meant a lot to him. Even during the COVID-19 shutdowns in early 2020, Boseman was still determined to do whatever work he could, even if he couldn't physically make hospital visits at the time. *Black Panther* executive producer Nate Moore revealed to *People* just how important that mission was to Boseman. The two worked together with Make-A-Wish, and at that particular time, they were planning how they could help make a child's wish come true despite the limitations. They were able to send the boy a voice message from Boseman and toys, and Moore noted it was Boseman who was determined to make sure the boy was able to get his wish.

Moore shared the last text message he received from Boseman, which read: "It broke me, man. But we need to do that for them. People deserve abundant life, special moments. They've been through hell battling disease. If we were able to ease their suffering and bring joy for a moment, and hopefully moments as he goes through the bags, then we made a difference in his life."

The executive producer also added his own thoughts on the text message after learning about Boseman's battle. "Again, hindsight will tell us that Chad felt that way because he too was battling a disease," he said to *People*. "But I don't think that's true. I think that's just who he was as a man. A leader and a caregiver first, who accomplished both of those things as a performer and as a regular person."

His claims definitely hold a lot of validity when it comes to the nature of Boseman's character. In an interview on SiriusXM, Boseman described just how much the cultural impact of *Black Panther* meant to him, especially when it came to children. He mentioned two boys he knew who had recently passed from cancer. And partly through his answer, he became so emotional that he was overcome with tears and had to pause for a moment.

He recalled in the interview, "Throughout our filming, I was communicating with them, knowing that they were both terminal…. Their parents said, 'They're trying to hold on til this movie comes.' And to a certain degree, you hear them say that and you're like, 'Wow, I gotta get up and go to the gym! I gotta get up and go to work. I gotta learn these lines. I gotta work on this accent.'… But to a certain degree, it's a humbling experience, because you're like, 'This can't mean that much to them.' You know? But seeing how the world has taken this on, seeing how the movement has taken on a life of its own… I realized that they anticipated something great."

Boseman thought about his own excitement as a kid when it came to birthdays and Christmas, so he could relate to just how special something like seeing *Black Panther* could be to those children. But the realization that they had passed was enough to make Boseman take a moment and collect his thoughts. He was soothed by his co-stars Danai Gurira and Lupita Nyong'o, and eventually he was able to regain his composure.

With Chadwick Boseman, you could see it was all real. He wore his heart on his sleeve, and he wouldn't let anything stop him from bringing a spark of joy in the lives of the children who needed it the most. But that wasn't all Boseman did to show how much he cared.

Giving Back

Viral videos and Chadwick Boseman seem to go hand-in-hand. And on one special occasion, Boseman had the help of late-night host Jimmy Fallon to pull it off.

Just after *Black Panther* was released in theaters, Fallon pulled together a special segment for *The Tonight Show Starring Jimmy Fallon*. Fallon invited a select number of people to come and talk about how much *Black Panther* meant to them. The filming room was unsuspecting, lined with red curtains and that velvet rope meant to look like they were getting the VIP treatment. And before them stood a large poster of Boseman as Black Panther, where they were meant to address their love of the film to Boseman. Well, Boseman on the poster, they thought.

Little did they know, Jimmy Fallon and *the* Chadwick Boseman were listening to their stories on the other side of the curtains. And just when the fans couldn't get more emotional from sharing their story, Boseman would step out to surprise every single one.

Among the participants was a young woman who was from Boseman's alma mater, Howard University. "I am so, so very proud to say that a Bison is T'Challa," she said, referring to the school's mascot. "Seriously, when you made your big scene when you came out, I shed a tear. It was a big deal for me, my friends, and definitely Howard University."

After all those years since graduation, Boseman was certainly making his university proud. So much so that he was the commencement speaker for Howard University's class of 2018. Boseman returned to Washington, D.C., that May to inspire the new generation of graduates. But his message was so universal that anybody in need of some inspiration could take the advice that Boseman gave out.

He started his speech recalling the time he ran into the late, great Muhammad Ali on campus one day. And then he recounted how his first gigs after

University Prep Academy High School students react to an announcement that all 600 students will see *Black Panther* on February 16, 2018, in Detroit. (AP Photo/Paul Sancya)

graduating from Howard went. While he had a successful theater career, it was a rocky start on screen. When he landed his major role in *All My Children*, he voiced his concern that the character would be too stereotypical. He was let go from the role (and soon-to-be co-star Michael B. Jordan actually replaced him), but he didn't let that stop him from pursuing his dreams in entertainment. He knew that just like Muhammad Ali, some days your fights will be victories and others will be losses. But you have to keep getting back up to fight. Never stay down.

For him, that fight wasn't just about finding your career. It was about finding your purpose. "Purpose is an essential element of you," he said in his speech. "It is the reason you are on the planet at this particular time in history. Your very existence is wrapped up in the things you are here to fulfill. Whatever you choose for a career path, remember, the struggles along the way are only meant to shape you for your purpose. When I dared to challenge the system that would relegate us to victims and stereotypes with no clear historical backgrounds, no hopes or talents, when I questioned that method of portrayal, a different path opened up for me, the path to my destiny."

Through his journey, we can see Boseman found his purpose in life. Yes, he was an actor and a writer and a director, but he found his true purpose when he began giving back to others. While these acts barely scratch the surface of all the good Chadwick Boseman was able to accomplish in his life, it does paint a beautiful picture of just how committed he was to giving back and making the world a brighter place while he could.

Chadwick Boseman, a Howard alumnus, receives an Honorary Doctorate Degree at the 2018 Howard University Commencement Ceremony at Howard University on May 12, 2018, in Washington, D.C. (Brian Stukes/Getty Images)

The World Honors a King

In the hours and days after the announcement of Chadwick Boseman's death, tributes and outpourings of grief flooded across the globe. Meanwhile, friends, colleagues, and admirers took to social media to share their thoughts and condolences. The following is merely a sampling of the enormous waves of emotion.

Letitia Wright

"A soul so beautiful, when you walked into a room, there was calm. You always moved with grace and ease… Every time I saw you, the world would be a better place…all that's left now is for us to allow all the seeds that you have planted on the earth to grow, to blossom, to become even more beautiful. You're forever in my heart."

Michael B. Jordan

"I'm more aware now than ever that time is short with people we love and admire. I'm gonna miss your honesty, your generosity, your sense of humor, and incredible gifts. I'll miss the gift of sharing space with you in scenes. I'm dedicating the rest of my days to live the way you did. With grace, courage, and no regrets. "Is this your king!?" Yes . he . is! Rest In Power Brother."

A Chadwick Boseman memorial at Howard University on August 31, 2020, in Washington, D.C. (Brian Stukes/Getty Images)

A man stops to shoot a picture of a mural memorializing Chadwick Boseman by artist Shane Grammer on September 8, 2020, in Los Angeles. (AP Photo/Chris Pizzello)

Ryan Coogler

"In African cultures, we often refer to loved ones that have passed on as ancestors. Sometimes you are genetically related. Sometimes you are not. I had the privilege of directing scenes of Chad's character, T'Challa, communicating with the ancestors of Wakanda. We were in Atlanta, in an abandoned warehouse, with bluescreens, and massive movie lights, but Chad's performance made it feel real. I think it was because, from the time that I met him, the ancestors spoke through him. It's no secret to me now how he was able to skillfully portray some of our most notable ones. I had no doubt that he would live on and continue to bless us with more. But it is with a heavy heart and a sense of deep gratitude to have ever been in his presence, that I have to reckon with the fact that Chad is an ancestor now. And I know that he will watch over us until we meet again."

Winston Duke

"Chadwick, you are the best...you are me and I'm you and we are all one! Thanks for being someone I could look up to on and off screen... your calm confidence was inspiring and exemplary. Thanks for sharing with me... you go ahead ...you did your job and did it well! You will NEVER be forgotten. Your heroism is now legend. We'll carry the load and honor your legacy, the rest of the way!"

Danai Gurira

"How do you honor a king? Reeling from the loss of my colleague, my friend, my brother. Struggling for words. Nothing feels adequate.... He made everyone feel loved, heard and seen. He played great, iconic roles because he possessed inside of himself that connection to greatness to be able to so richly bring them to life. He had a heroic spirit, and marched to the beat of his own drum; hence his excellence as an artist and the incredible courage and determination as he faced life's challenges; while still guiding us all."

Bob Iger

"He brought enormous strength, dignity and depth to his groundbreaking role of Black Panther; shattering myths and stereotypes, becoming a long-awaited hero to millions around the world, and inspiring us all to dream bigger and demand more than the status quo. We mourn all that he was, as well as everything he was destined to become."

Robert Downey Jr.

"Mr. Boseman leveled the playing field while fighting for his life… That's heroism… I'll remember the good times, the laughter, and the way he changed the game."

Kevin Feige

"Chadwick's passing is absolutely devastating. He was our T'Challa, our Black Panther, and our dear friend. Each time he stepped on set, he radiated charisma and joy, and each time he appeared on screen, he created something truly indelible. He embodied a lot of amazing people in his work, and nobody was better at bringing great men to life. He was as smart and kind and powerful and strong as any person he portrayed. Now he takes his place alongside them as an icon for the ages."

Chris Evans

"I'm absolutely devastated. This is beyond heartbreaking. Chadwick was special. A true original. He was a deeply committed and constantly curious artist. Few performers have such power and versatility. He had so much amazing work still left to create. I'm endlessly grateful for our friendship. My thoughts and prayers are with his family. Rest in power, King."

Angela Bassett

"This young man's dedication was awe-inspiring, his smile contagious, his talent unreal. So I pay tribute to a beautiful spirit, a consummate artist, a soulful brother… 'thou aren't not dead but flown afar…' All you possessed, Chadwick, you freely gave. Rest now, sweet prince. #WakandaForever."

Black Panther fan Keyon Griffin poses for a portrait during a Chadwick Boseman tribute on September 3, 2020, in Anderson, South Carolina. (AP Photo/ Brynn Anderson)

Brie Larson

"Chadwick was someone who radiated power and peace. Who stood for so much more than himself. Who took the time to really see how you were doing and gave words of encouragement when you felt unsure. I'm honored to have the memories I have. The conversations, the laughter. My heart is with you and your family. You will be missed and never forgotten. Rest in power and peace my friend."

Dwayne Johnson

"This was hard to hear about. Hard to imagine the quiet pain and struggle you went thru all these years, yet still shined your powerful light and talents to inspire the world. Especially, our kids who finally saw themselves as a superhero—because of you."

Jamie Foxx

"Please Jesus please… I know you know what's best… but at this moment our hearts are writhing with so much pain… so to lose this beautiful black king renders me weak… please watch over his family and loved ones… @chadwickboseman you have touched the lives of all of us… u will forever be remembered in the highest regard… REST IN POWER! our black king! Our black panther!"

Joe Biden

"The true power of Chadwick Boseman was bigger than anything we saw on screen. From the Black Panther to Jackie Robinson, he inspired generations and showed them they can be anything they want— even super heroes. Jill and I are praying for his loved ones at this difficult time."

Kamala Harris

"Heartbroken. My friend and fellow Bison Chadwick Boseman was brilliant, kind, learned, and humble. He left too early but his life made a difference. Sending my sincere condolences to his family."

Halle Berry

"Here's to an incredible man with immeasurable talent, who leaned into life regardless of his personal battles. You never truly know what the people around you might be going through—treat them with kindness and cherish every minute you have together."

A passerby looks at a mural honoring Chadwick Boseman in Rio de Janeiro on September 2, 2020. (Mauro Pimentel/AFP via Getty Images)

Mark Ruffalo

"All I have to say is the tragedies amassing this year have only been made more profound by the loss of #ChadwickBoseman. What a man, and what an immense talent. Brother, you were one of the all time greats and your greatness was only beginning. Lord love ya. Rest in power, King."

Cicely Tyson

"God of our silent tears! A brilliant & talented actor, gone too soon. @chadwickboseman you leave this earth w/a beautiful body of work. When you graced our screens you brought the dignity & grace we could all be proud of. My prayers are with your loving family."

Oprah Winfrey

"What a gentle gifted SOUL. Showing us all that Greatness in between surgeries and chemo. The courage, the strength, the Power it takes to do that. This is what Dignity looks like."

Sterling K. Brown

"I don't have words. Rest In Peace, Bruh. Thank you for all you did while you were here. Thank you for being a friend. You are loved. You will be missed."

Zoe Saldana

"You were one of the classiest men I have ever met in my life. It was an honor to have shared minutes with you on screen and to have crossed paths with you during press. Though our acquaintance was light you always left a lasting impression because of your energy, poise and gentle manner. May the Universe deliver you to your promise land brother."

Disney's El Capitan Theatre honors Chadwick Boseman on its marquee on September 10, 2020, in Los Angeles. (AaronP/Bauer-Griffin/GC Images)

Barack Obama

"Chadwick came to the White House to work with kids when he was playing Jackie Robinson. You could tell right away that he was blessed. To be young, gifted, and Black; to use that power to give them heroes to look up to; to do it all while in pain—what a use of his years."

Michelle Obama

"I'll always remember watching Chadwick in *42*. Barack and I were alone in the White House, on a weekend night with the girls away. I was so profoundly moved by the rawness and emotion in the barrier-breaking story. And not long after, when he came to meet with young people in the State Dining Room, I saw that Chadwick's brilliance on screen was matched by a warmth and sincerity in person.

"There's a reason he could play Jackie Robinson, Thurgood Marshall, and King T'Challa with such captivating depth and honesty. He, too, knew what it meant to truly persevere. He, too, knew that real strength starts inside. And he, too, belongs right there with them as a hero—for Black kids and for all of our kids. There's no better gift with which to grace our world."

LeBron James crosses his arms for the Wakanda salute during a moment of silence to honor Chadwick Boseman on August 29, 2020, in Lake Buena Vista, Florida. (Kevin C. Cox/Getty Images)

CHADWICK BO
1976 - 202

The Los Angeles Clippers kneel to pay respect to the Black Lives Matters movement while a photo of Chadwick Boseman is displayed on a screen behind them on August 30, 2020, in Lake Buena Vista, Florida. (AP Photo/Ashley Landis)